BELIEVE
IN
Your Purpose

BELIEVE
IN
Your Purpose

A Guide to
Becoming a Successful
Purpose-Driven Entrepreneur

SHANNON WILKERSON

© 2018 by Shannon Wilkerson

Believe in Your Purpose: *A Guide to Becoming a Successful Purpose-Driven Entrepreneur*

Published by ZION Publishing House

Sioux Falls, S. D. & Washington, D. C.

www.zionpublishinghouse.com

ISBN: 978-1-7323520-6-3 print

ISBN: 978-1-7323520-5-6 eBook

All rights reserved. The author guarantees all contents are original and do not infringe upon the legal rights of any other person or work. No part of this book may be reproduced, distributed, or transmitted in any form or by any means –electronic, mechanical, digital, photocopy, recording, or any other—except for brief quotations in printed reviews, without the prior written permission of the publisher.

Scripture taken from the New King James Version®. Copyright © 1982 by Thomas Nelson. Used by permission. All rights reserved.

Scripture taken from the Holy Bible, NEW INTERNATIONAL VERSION®, NIV® Copyright © 1973, 1978, 1984, 2011 by Biblica, King Inc.® Used by permission. All rights reserved worldwide.

PRINTED IN THE UNITED STATES OF AMERICA

This book is dedicated to my mother who believed in my dream to be an author, even as a child, and to all my sister-friends who have listened to me talk about writing this book for three years without even writing one sentence. You didn't lose enthusiasm for this project and have been a great encouragement to me. You are invaluable!

Contents

Prologue	ix
Introduction	xi
Chapter 1 Who Are You	1
Identifying Your Purpose and Gifts	6
Lost Dreams	9
Avoid Money Traps	10
Use What's in Your Hands	12
Chapter 2 The Mind Shift	17
Make Space to do Business	21
What's the Message?	26
Chapter 3 Commitment to the Journey	35
Stop Switching Up	41
Vision Boards and Journaling	44
Chapter 4 Push	53
When Purpose Shifts	57
A Closed Door	60
Chapter 5 Connections that Count	65
Forming Your Circle of Support	66
The Approach to Forming Your Circle of Support	70
Be an Opportunist	71
Everyone is Not For You	73
Accountability	77

Chapter 6 It's Not Just You	81
When Your Family and Friends Don't Support You	83
To Leave or Not to Leave?	87
Chapter 7 The Invisible Business	93
Sharing vs. Selling	98
Why You're Really Afraid to Tell People About Your Business	100
Bonus Chapter	105
Becoming a Woman of Purpose	106
All the Single Ladies	109
A Final Word	112

Prologue: This is for YOU!

It was an amazing experience writing this book. I had suffered from writer's block for years and nothing seemed to work to bring forth this gift that I knew I had. It wasn't until I started this project, I realized that, in reality, my "writer's block" was God telling me that I was not focused on or writing about the right thing! What I put in this book will guide you through the process of realizing your purpose and being able to walk it out in a big way. You will get the keys to be a successful purpose-driven entrepreneur, but you have to do the work and utilize those keys to unlock it for yourself. You will also get practical tips and strategies for networking, marketing, and bringing purpose to your business. No matter where you are in your entrepreneurship journey, this book is for you!

Sincerely,

Shannon

x

Introduction

Still trying to figure out if this book is for you…..

I had been a Business Coach for a few years and had met so many women with awesome ideas and amazing gifts on the inside of them. It was an honor to meet and work with these women. There was however, one thing that bothered me. Many of them felt unsupported in their ventures to start businesses and live out their dreams. I could see that this was doing something to their level of confidence, which in turn had been affecting their level of success. They were discovering that sometimes their friends and family were not as supportive as they would like, and sometimes doors were closing in their faces. I wanted to help them to see that they still must go on!

Like myself, they had also been to seminars and meetings presented by "Coaches" promising to provide tips and tools that would lead them into their best life and leaving disappointed because all they got was a sales pitch. They expressed feeling like all anybody was ever interested in was getting their money. I have been there and done that, and I can't tell you how much money I have spent. They were not getting what they needed as a new entrepreneur and had been feeling let down by those closest to them, as well as other women in business. It was from those conversations that I decided to write this book and to work more with women on a mission to living their purpose, which begins with believing that you have everything it takes to be successful.

The way that we visualize ourselves in our wildest dreams are not just far-fetched fantasies of what life could have been like for us if not for this or that unfortunate event that took place in our lives. They are images, ideas, and thoughts purposefully placed in our hearts by God Himself to express the life that He wants for us and the gifts that He has given us freely.

> *"For I know the plans I have for you,"* declares the Lord, *"plans to prosper you and not to harm you, plans to give you hope and a future,"* Jeremiah 29:11 (New International Version).

God wants us to dream big. In fact, He wants us to dream bigger than ourselves, so we recognize that we need Him in order to accomplish those things that we dream. God wants us to reach a place of walking out His perfect plan for our lives even if it isn't exactly what we planned for ourselves, and even if nobody goes with us for the journey. What's on the inside of you waiting for you to stop being afraid to carry out? Who and what is waiting for you to believe in your purpose?

My #1 goal for this book is not only to inspire you, but also to set you up for success by providing the "how to." Being inspired is one thing. Knowing what's next is the key. Reaching success is not this mysterious thing reserved for just a few of us. It is readily available to anyone who will put in the work and do the steps. If you are not yet willing and motivated, your dream may not be big enough and may lack purpose to back it up.

In each chapter of this book, you will be challenged to reflect and evaluate your thoughts. These thoughts will become your words and then your actions! You will be challenged to do something different in order to obtain a different result. These are important steps to being able to manifest your dreams. You will also get valuable and practical tips that you can apply immediately to see progress today in your current situation as it relates to giving your business a boost. I'm giving you the tools and unlocking the mystery that you thought was only for "those people."

Please enjoy my book, but at the same time, take it very seriously. It can be just another book to you or "that book"—that book that was so real and spoke to you on so many levels, that you couldn't be the same after you read it. Yes, that book!

Chapter One
Who Are You?

Who are you? Seems like a weird question, right? You would be surprised at how many women can't answer that question without mentioning the roles that they play. For example, when asked, they might say, "I am a mom," or "I am a business owner." Ok, but what else? If I stripped away all of your roles, who would be left?

Knowing who you are is the absolute number one step in identifying your purpose and beginning to plan for a business that reflects that purpose, your passions, and your character. The world doesn't need another business created just for generating income. What the world needs is more leaders who are willing to step up with boldness and live in their purpose to create a better situation for themselves and for others. That starts within you. We all have the strength within ourselves to achieve and fulfil our purpose. We just have to tap into that strength.

Earlier this year, I hosted a workshop for women in business. At the beginning of the session, I asked the women to describe themselves in three words. Immediately, many of them looked nervous as if they did not know what to say. I could feel the tension as everyone hoped I wouldn't ask them to speak. As I called on each one, they struggled and started to name their roles. I explained to them that the task at hand should be easy because nobody knows *you like you do*.

If I stripped away all of your roles, who would be left?

Describing yourself should be simple. One of the ladies admitted it was difficult to describe herself because it was something she doesn't think about regularly. Her mind is usually consumed by what she has to do every day (the roles that she plays) and other people like her husband, children, and elderly parents. It is so easy to fall into this trap because we all have responsibilities and people who depend on us. That's ok. However, we must not lose sight of our purpose. If we do, we will soon resent those people and will blame them because we did not accomplish our life goals. They would be held responsible even though we ourselves would be to blame for our own life choices.

I will be the first to admit that sometimes you have to dig deep to find yourself in the midst of all of the noise, distractions, and responsibilities that we face daily. Let me tell you, you are more than a mother to your children, a wife to your husband, a caregiver, a CEO, etc. Those are wonderful roles to walk in. However, you were born with a purpose that goes far beyond all of that. God has placed some things on the inside of you that are buried under motherhood, being a good wife, working too many hours, and taking care of everything and everyone around you.

Are you the one family member who everyone depends on? I am. I spent years catering to everyone. Whenever anyone needed anything, my phone ring. I was a taxi driver, a babysitter, a grocery store shopper, etc. Once I became a business coach, everyone in my world who desired to be in business wanted free advice. Everybody wanted the service, but nobody wanted to pay for it. Sound familiar? I struggled, and to be honest, I sometimes still struggle to tell people, "No." However, I am a lot better at it now after years of constantly going through drama with people who totally inconvenienced me with no regard for my time. Now, I know how to take time to work on my own personal goals and do not allow others to interrupt that time. Guess what? *When I was done, everyone was still alive.* Nobody met a fatal end because I could not address their need immediately. This is how I progress, and if you want to progress, it will require you do the same.

Another woman in this workshop commented that she was hesitant to say good things about herself because she didn't want to sound full of herself. I laughed, inwardly, of course. I am so full of myself, it's unbelievable! If I don't think highly of myself, who else will? I am the daughter of a King! I am the best thing since sliced bread, and nobody on this earth can tell me this is not true! Does this mean that I don't think other people are just as amazing? No. I absolutely do and absolutely love to see other people shine. I am just fully aware of my own shine.

We must not be caught up in how others perceive us. Yes, we should strive for excellence and want to be seen in a positive light at all times, but if someone doesn't see that because they are blinded by jealousy or a lack of self-love, we continue on. Never make yourself small to make someone else feel better in your own space. Instead, help them to see the beauty and the strength in themselves. Self-love is the key to being able to love and appreciate other people because you feel no need to compete with them.

Discovering who you really are and your purpose, requires a certain level of getting to know yourself. Sounds silly, right? A lot of people aren't comfortable being alone with their own thoughts. These are the people who you will see who have to always have the TV or radio on or some other background distraction. They rarely take time to just sit and think. We need *thinking time*. We also need prayer time. It is in this time, you get to know you, what God has for you, and how to attract it to your life. If you are not getting this time in, you are missing out on opportunities to receive a download from heaven that will change your life and set you on a new path.

Identifying Your Purpose & Gifts

Take a moment to think about who you really are. I guarantee it will lead you to your purpose. I am a teacher. I have always been a teacher. When my younger sister was born, I was four years old and took on the responsibility of teaching her everything that I knew in my rapidly growing four-year-old brain. I was a pretty good teacher too, even then, because she started kindergarten with all of the necessary skills to excel based on what I taught her. As I grew, I would line up stuffed animals and dolls on my bed and teach them. I played "school" for years at playtime at home even before I had ever been in a real school myself.

When I entered school, I was always the teacher's helper. I helped teach other children who struggled with things that came easy for me. When I got to high school and it was time to choose elective courses, I chose child development. It was a three-year program which gave me the opportunity to work with preschool children who were brought to my high school the first year, to intern at an elementary school the second year, and to work in a preschool, for pay, the third year. I was so excited to have three years of half-day schedules, and my career path was set. I knew exactly what I planned to do after high school. I graduated and went into an Early Childhood Education program in college.

After a long career in the field of education working with children, I started teaching adults who worked with children and wanted to open child care sites and preschool centers. This led to a career in business coaching. In addition to that, today, I teach through speaking engagements to various audiences of educators and business owners.

I have also been writing since I was five years old. There are crazy, embarrassing audio tapes and maybe even some VHS tapes circulating of me creating and singing songs and telling stories at this age. Of course, my older sister was right there encouraging me so that she could have something to tease me with later. In elementary school, I won a contest and had a poem that I wrote published called, "My Grandmother Prayed for Me."

My purpose and passions were always present even as a child. If you listen to those who are thriving in any industry, most times they will have a similar story to share about knowing at an early age what they were destined to become. I'm sure you've heard really great singers and entertainers say they started out singing in the children's choir at church or comedians describing themselves as class clowns in school.

If you look at the children in your life right now, you will likely recognize their gifts right away. That is God showing you a clear path for them. Please nurture and encourage them and give them every opportunity to grow in that area. It will make all the difference in their future. If you were fortunate enough for someone to have done this for you, you know how valuable it is. If not, it's not too late to tap into your purpose. It is still a God-given gift. That has not changed.

Identifying your purpose is like identifying how you will touch others and change the world we live in. We all have something within us that is meant to be used to enrich the lives of others. So many people allow this to go to waste, and as a result, many others suffer until someone else comes along and decides to walk *it* out. Don't wait for someone else. Be that someone else! There are specific people waiting for you. You are the person they will be able to connect with and create change.

Lost Dreams

Think about your childhood. For this moment, let's not focus on any trauma you may have faced at this delicate point of your life. Let's focus only on our dreams. What did you dream about? Did you want to be a doctor or maybe an actress? How did you see yourself then, and is that what you see now? Are you still working on meeting your goals, or have you completely forgotten about them? If you've forgotten about them, why? Did you think it was too big of a dream to actually live? Did you not have the tools to carry it out? Did you get married and take a break from your dreams to have a family? Why not pick it back up again, but this time, run with it! Don't waste your talent.

Even though I knew I had a gift to write, I had not really written anything in many years because I was too consumed by life events to even focus or to have a creative thought. Do you ever feel like that? Do you ever feel so bogged down with mess that you can't think, focus, or use your gift, or walk in your purpose? Think about your day to day routines. If I could be a fly on the wall, would I see you just surviving, or working toward living your best life? Do you find yourself thinking mostly about bills or goals?

Avoid Money Traps

At one point in my life, I was definitely thinking about bills more than anything. I guess that goes hand in hand with not having enough money to pay them. You have to think about your bills when they are more than your income. Not getting your money right, will hinder your goals because you won't be able to give them the focus it takes to make things happen. You'll be too consumed with survival. Also, many of our goals will require an investment. Notice, I did not say our goals will cost money. I said they will require an investment because I believe that money will return to you, plus a lot more, when you invest it properly.

Many of us have or have had money issues because of our relationship to money. How we feel about and utilize money is usually based on our circumstances growing up. I wasn't always a saver. I come from a single-parent, paycheck-to-paycheck, working overtime household. If I wanted things, I had to wait for them until another paycheck came. As a result, if I got a lump sum of money as an adult, I would put half of it toward paying off debt, which was good, but the other half would be freely given to department stores. I no longer wanted to wait for what I wanted. I would just buy it if I had the money in my hand.

Spending frivolously may not be an issue for some people. However, they may not make a lot of money and not really know how to manage money in a way which will allow them to save even with a tiny budget. Daily expenses are so high that many families can't see how they can save or invest money. They are more concerned about eating and paying rent. Falling into either one of these money traps, will hinder your progress in business, because again, doing business requires an investment. Also, not having a grasp on how to handle money, will really mess you up once you really start making more money. More money does not necessarily mean fewer financial problems.

I encourage you to get smart about money. If necessary, consult a professional. There are free resources available to assist you with this. There are also books that will teach you how to invest and save. This is something you can take advantage of regardless of how much money you have today. I have definitely taken full advantage of all of the literature available and have made great strides in this area of my life. Don't be one of the people with a $3,000 handbag and $500 in your savings account. We all know a couple people like this.

Use What's in Your Hands

Have you ever considered ways that you could use your purpose or gift to get your finances right in order to fund a business? I know far too many women who are really gifted and talented and have so much purpose on the inside of them, they are currently hiding. I often hear the excuse that they don't have the necessary resources to do what they really want to do, so they just do nothing. It is much better to start something than to just sit on your gift.

If your gift is cooking, you probably enjoy cooking for the people you love. How about getting paid to do that? I'm not saying to stop cooking for free for your loved ones and start charging your children for dinner plates, but if your loved ones want you to cook for a hundred people at a baby shower or wedding reception, you should be paid! You could then use that money to get your finances in order, increase your credit score by paying off debt, and qualify for a business loan to open up your own restaurant. Heck, you could even open it with your own cash if you do well enough. Just some food for thought.

If you are wonderful with children, offer babysitting services for date nights for friends and family. Save your extra earnings to put toward starting a child care business or a nanny placement service. You could even open a family child care site in your home and save up for a larger site. Most things happen in steps. You have to be prepared to walk this thing all the way out.

Regardless of what your purpose is, in order to discover and walk in it, you have to spend quiet time with God and be able to hear and see what He is saying to you. Hearing, but not being able to see it due to nonbelief, is what stumps a lot of people. For example; if God says you will be a millionaire, and right now you don't have enough money to cover your rent, you may not be able to see yourself as a millionaire. You don't yet believe it. As a result, unfortunately, you will never get there unless that changes. When your purpose is revealed to you, you have to be able to see it. Visualize yourself walking that thing out. This visualization will give you something to work toward. You have a vision for your life, and you can now move in that direction.

What is the thing you do better than most other people? What are you passionate about? Are you great at interior decorating and design? Do you do a great job motivating other people? Do people love to come to your house to eat? Why is this thing not creating a paycheck for you? Why are you not using your gifts to create the life you want to live? There are few things more satisfying than waking up every day and doing the

When your purpose is revealed to you, you have to be able to see it.

one thing you love to do. Actually, getting paid for it is just icing on the cake!

Never underestimate your gifts and talents. You may be surprised at the things other people will pay you for. Because of my experience in early childhood education, I have been paid to help a family select a child care site for their children, to create lesson plans for a mom who was home-schooling, and to child-proof a home, etc. I have a friend who was paid to teach a teenager how to do laundry and organize his room. She now has a cleaning and organizing business.

Purpose-Driven Steps

- Describe yourself without using titles or roles
- Identify your purpose, gifts, and talents
- Document ways you can use your purpose to impact others

Chapter 2
The Mind Shift

Your purpose is not small. It may seem that way in comparison to what someone else is doing, but always remember your gift fills a need and is just as important as the gifts that you observe in others. You just need to stay in your lane and do what God has called you to do. When it is time for you to expand your lane, do it especially if you are not happy with where you are. Living beneath your potential is not fun. Feeling stuck there is much worse. However, you should value where you are as a step in your journey. You should be able to enjoy each phase as God elevates you more and more.

I met a woman last year named Stephanie who was a child care provider. She had a small family childcare site in her home with eight children. She was providing care for children from mostly low-income working families. Her child care rate was much lower than the market rate in order to accommodate these families, and she often went above and beyond in providing for these children. She would feed them dinner before they left, buy clothes, socks, diapers, or anything else if she saw there was a need and that the parents were struggling. I thought she was amazing! The parents really appreciated her, and the children loved her.

During a visit to her daycare, I commented on how wonderful I thought she was, and how she was serving her community in such a big way. Her response to me was "It's just what I knew I had to do. It's no big deal." I, immediately, corrected her and explained that it was a huge deal! She is making a difference in the lives of these eight families and spreading love in a way that they may not experience anywhere else. I also explained to her how honored I was to be in her presence, and how delighted I had been to receive an invite to see her program. She continued, "There isn't much to see here." She had been feeding herself the lie for so long that she wasn't as awesome as she was. It became my new job to make her see! She was so used to belittling herself and making comparisons between what she was doing and what large chain child-care programs were doing. However, her service matters, and she truly has a purpose in the community and a gift in serving families.

It's ok to want to do more than what you are currently doing, but we must shift our minds to see what we are already doing as valuable. Believe it or not, this will become the necessary motivation to do more. I worked with her for over a year. She has moved her business out of her home and now has a small child-care center serving twelve families and receives government money to help support her business and to continue to keep her fees low. She is able to provide even more for the children and families in her care. As a result, these children's lives are greatly enriched. Her

It's ok to want to do more than what you are currently doing, but we must shift our minds to see what we are already doing as valuable.

goal is to open a center that she can fill with over one hundred children. I don't think she would ever have that as a goal if she were not first able to see how much of a difference she was making in people's lives, or if she was motivated only by money. Many more families will receive her love and benefit from her generosity in the future.

Like Stephanie, your purpose is big and will touch many more people if you allow it. Don't let small thinking hold you back from being awesome! If you think small, you will act small, and your asking will be small. What do I mean by that? When you pray and ask God to move on your behalf, what are you asking for? Are you asking just for a bill to be paid so that your business can live to see another month, or are you asking for supernatural increase in clients or customers so that you can go to the next level? Do you have the confidence in your purpose to ask like that? When you meet potential clients, are you talking about your business in a way that will attract them to buy from you, or are you timid and thinking, "They won't want my product."? If you think that, they won't; trust me.

Make Space to do Business

Once you make up your mind that you have a purpose, you have to clear out the clutter and make space for it. Deciding to be dedicated to starting a business of purpose is a huge undertaking. When you start out, keep in mind that this is something new. It hasn't always been a part of your life. So, you have to make space physically, mentally, and emotionally for this. It's like when you are expecting a child. You prepared a room, bought supplies, and maybe made some lifestyle changes to get ready for the birth. Well, now you are birthing your purpose! That takes preparation as well.

So, you wake up one morning and decide, "I am going to give this a go!" For me, this day was a super important milestone that I will never forget. I had all of these wonderful ideas in my mind and started to make a bunch of plans for turning these ideas into a business. I was super goal focused and ready to jump right in, in that moment. Then the phone rang, emails started coming in, people were texting me requesting this or that, and my mind went right back to my "real life." Incorporating my dreams, goals, and purpose was not yet a part of my real life. It was just in my head, and my real life was still happening around me.

That evening, feeling defeated because I had not done anything with my ideas that day, I laid in my bed thinking about how I could do things differently the next day. I wrote down everything I wanted to do and scheduled it in. I went to sleep ready to take on the next day in a big way. When I woke up, I took my list off the night stand and started to read it. Before I even finished reading it, the same thing happened that occurred the day before. Another day went by with no progress.

On the third day I got smart. I realized that in order to make space to work on my purpose, I had to eliminate some other things that were in the way. When you get to this place, my recommendation is that you focus on the external things first, which for some can be the easiest thing to tackle. Clear out physical clutter, first. I am a neat freak. So, I was able to pretty much skip this step. If you can't say the same, get working on it. Create a space in your home where you can work purposefully. Remove the clutter from this space and add the things you will need to be productive. For me this included the basics: pens, paper, sticky notes, highlighters, etc. I also added a lemongrass candle, which is great for productivity, a comfortable chair, and flowers on my desk. I replaced my flowers weekly to make my space more inviting. On the wall behind my desk, was a visual display of my current goals. I placed my desk right by my bedroom window because it overlooked a little courtyard with the most beautiful roses. I had all the sunlight and scenery that I could take. It was a great place to sit, especially in the mornings.

Next, I had to eliminate the noise. I had to train myself to leave the television off and to have more quiet time to think, and as I said before, to hear from God. I also had to silence my cell phone to stop the text alerts and phone calls. To make sure I was sticking to this, I added a chart to the wall that included all the daily tasks that I could not eliminate and marked uninterrupted time for my business. At one point, I had an alarm set in my phone to remind me it was time to work on my goals.

    I will be honest and say this last part was the most difficult. I had to free myself emotionally in order to walk in my purpose. I had to make space in my heart for my purpose. We have all had life experiences, some good and some bad. A lot of women that I have met have been held back by these experiences. The good experiences have taught them that in order for things to be good, it should come in a specific way, (i.e.) wrapped with a pretty bow just the way you like it. This is the cause of many missed blessings. The bad experiences have taught them to be fearful and unsure of themselves or have damaged their self-esteem. Both scenarios can be a hindrance to your success. You may block or turn your back on success because it's not packaged how you thought it should be. Or, you may be too fearful to pursue your goals consistently and be unable to bounce back after disappointment or rejection.

    My issue was I was always concerned about what others would say and how they would receive me. I was also very afraid of failure. What would people think of me if I failed? This was holding me back a lot.

It made me keep quiet about my goals. I had secret goals because if nobody knew about them, I wouldn't be embarrassed if I didn't accomplish them. Can I have a secret business and be successful at it? I can't, and neither can you. I had to ask God to show me the root of these fears, so I could deal with them.

As a child, I was teased by classmates mostly for being too skinny. This hurt my feelings and created emotional scars and insecurities that I didn't need to have because as I see now, I have always been a beautiful girl! I just could not see that then. These insecurities led to low self-esteem. As an adult, well-meaning older adults in my life saw me working diligently, as an entrepreneur, and would say things like, "You just need to get a good job to retire from." That made me question if I was doing the right thing, or did I just need to get a job and secure a retirement check. I was insecure about my decision. I had to settle it within myself that I was in the will of God for my life and that I would stand firm in my decision. After all, how can someone who knows very little about what I am doing tell me what I need to do? I had to learn to walk in complete confidence in myself and what I was doing, understanding that I was exactly where I was supposed to be in this season of my life, and doing exactly what I was supposed to be doing. Period.

I don't know what your one thing is that may be holding you back, or if you have more than one thing.

Everyone has a unique situation. The good thing is God is familiar with all of your situations, and deliverance is available to us all! Take that thing to Him and ask God to walk you through the process of letting it go and moving on so that you can be your own kind of wonderful! Otherwise, it will continue to show up in your life and continue to cost you. If you need counseling, get it. If you need a support group, join one. Do whatever it is you need to do to be better, and don't worry about what people will have to say about it.

What's the Message?

Once you have made some physical and head space to do business, you have to decide on the messages you want to put out there to the world. It is critical that you do this long before you ever speak to anyone about your business because this will guide all your interactions as you venture out. Consider the type of experiences you want people to have as they connect to your business and what you want to stand out in the consumer's mind when they think about you or your product. This is called your *brand message*. Your brand message may be expressed in a tag line on your website, but it is much more than that. As I said before, it will guide what you say to potential clients and how you do business in general.

A good starting place to describe your brand message would be to identify your core values. What

A good starting place to describe your brand message would be to identify your core values.

do you stand for? What is your purpose? This is different for most every business. My purpose is to guide entrepreneurs into developing businesses that will fulfill their purpose and also provide financial independence, of course. I must then consider my target audience and what is important to them. My target audience is women entrepreneurs and based on surveys that I have conducted, I know that financial independence and having more time to spend with their families are two very important factors for this audience.

Armed with this information, I have developed my brand message: for women to utilize their purpose to create wealth. I don't say it exactly like that in those words each time, but that is the consistent message. This message will resonate with my target audience because it was developed with them in mind. Whenever I am invited as a speaker for an event, I am pushing this message. This message is expressed on my website and social media pages. When I have conversations with people, I leave them with a very clear impression of what I stand for and who I am. Everywhere that you see my business, you receive this same message.

If you've done business for any length of time or been to any networking event, I am sure you have heard the term, "elevator pitch." This is a quick thirty-sixty second description of your business meant to capture the attention of your target audience quickly.

You should be able to describe the value your company offers in such a way that will persuade a potential client or customer to want to learn more in the time that it takes for the elevator to reach their floor. You should practice this! You never know when you will need it. It should express your brand message and key benefits to doing business with you. Be ready at all times! That is the biggest piece of advice I can give to any entrepreneur.

    I attended a networking event some years ago when I was just recently starting out doing workshops for educators. During lunch, I was approached by a woman who I did not know, at the time, was a director of a preschool with six sites in my state. She asked me what I did in the field. My answer was short and not very descriptive at all. I just said, "I train teachers at various preschool centers in MD, DC, and VA, as well as a few elementary schools in MD." She shook her head and said, "That's interesting." We sat in silence for about ten seconds, and then someone else grabbed her attention and pulled her away. She was gone in less than two minutes.

    This could have been a missed opportunity. I was not prepared to share my message with her, lacked the confidence to share with her, and my mind was on food at the moment. This was a bad combination. This was a connection I needed to make. This was a woman who I needed to make an impression on because she had the potential to increase my income quite a bit. How many times have you left money on the table? How many times have you missed an opportunity to share your purpose?

I was blessed that a client later, during the event, brought this woman back over to me and did an introduction. She had not known we had met earlier. She said, "This is our program trainer, Shannon Wilkerson. She is an excellent trainer and has made great strides within our program with our teachers. They are managing their classrooms a lot better, the children are doing better on assessments, and my program, as a whole, has grown since she has been with us." In about thirty seconds, she sealed the deal for me. I got a three-year contract that day. She did my elevator pitch for me. At that time, she knew something I did not. Thank God for grace! That would have been a huge loss.

The main obstacle that stops us from having the confidence to share our brand message is that we can lack confidence in our own brand! That comes from jumping in too quickly and poor planning. If you knew you had the best product on the market, and you had done everything in excellence, you would be so proud and would always be ready to share about it. Unfortunately, if you are not proud of your product, it becomes apparent, and that lack of confidence and excellence is what becomes your brand message. A lack of professionalism and preparation is memorable. We don't soon forget bad experiences with a business. Having a reputation for dropping the ball is a confidence killer.

I have made several attempts to support small businesses and been let down in a big way. I have had interactions with business owners who do not follow up on conversations, do not follow through with what they promised, or produced work I was not happy with at all. I have even experienced not being able to support a small business because I could not find links to their website, or the website wasn't professionally done and was confusing to read. I spent my money elsewhere because I don't have time to deal with stuff like that. If you didn't have time to get your business in order, why should I make time to try to figure you out? Most people are looking for something quick and easy and will not take the time to figure your mess out in order to give you money. As small business owners, we must keep in mind, we should operate our business as professionals. Though we are called a small business, our businesses are big deals, and unfortunately, people are way more critical of us.

Your business is so important. Its success is linked to you being able to live in your purpose. Take time to create a business you can be proud of and then protect it. This includes being mindful of what you do online even on your personal social media pages. I can't tell you how many times I have decided not to work with someone because of the garbage they posted online. It does not matter that it is your personal page. People are still looking, and you never know how many people on your personal friends' list may want to do business with you but won't because you are a little too "free" online.

Invest in professional marketing tools, including photos. This will give you a professional look, and people will take you seriously. Keep your brand images consistent. Your website, business cards, social media pages, t-shirt, etc. should all match. People need to be able to recognize your business across all platforms. Using varying colors and styles will confuse people and could cause you to lose business if the consumer is not sure he or she is dealing with the same person. It also makes you look wishy washy.

Develop content for your website that will capture the attention of and engage your intended audience. Online consumers have a short attention span. If you don't grab their attention immediately, they are on to the next best thing. If content development is not a strength of yours, you need to invest in having a professional to get the job done. This is an added investment that will be well worth it. Your online presence will be most people's first interaction with your business. Make a lasting and positive impression.

Purpose-Driven Steps

- Consider the things that you do and have thought of as insignificant. Think about and write how you can use those talents, gifts, and passions to contribute to your own success and the success of others.

- Write down emotional and mental hurt or stress that you need to deal with in order to step into entrepreneurship successfully.

- Create your brand message and key benefits to others who may want to do business with you.

- Develop your elevator pitch.

34 | Page Believe in Your Purpose

Chapter 3

Committed to the Journey

I have been handed so many business cards from entrepreneurs with businesses that are no longer around. Why is that? There are several reasons why this is the case, but for some, it is simply because their business venture was just about money. You can always tell when a person is in love with what they do, and when it's all about the dollar. Your experience with them will be much different because their commitment level is much different. When something is not connected to who you are and why you are here in this world, you are willing to let go of it without much of a struggle. I know all about that because I have been guilty of this myself. The business I am currently in is not my first attempt at business. I thank God for the ability to learn from mistakes and to not repeat them.

In 2012, I was approached by several girlfriends who had signed up with a popular Multi-Level Marketing (MLM) company selling health and wellness products. This is so not my thing, but I signed up after being asked by three different friends. I even hosted a few parties at my home and used the products myself. I was able to get some loyal customers and sell products at events with no problem. However, I was not growing within the business like other people were. Why? Because, I did not care about the business. It was a means to additional income, and that's all. I had no passion or purpose behind joining this company. Yes, I wanted to be healthy and wanted others to be healthy also, but I did not want to sell these products.

After about a year, I cancelled my account with the MLM and was stuck with a closet full of products I ended up giving away to friends and family. In this process I learned two things about myself. One, I am not good at doing things that are not connected to my life passions. Two, I don't want to be a pushy sales person and have to chase down money. I would much rather do what I love and let the money follow me. I had to learn, when you are doing something purposeful, clients will be attracted to you. I can honestly say I have never had to work to get clients as a business coach. I had to put in my work to make sure I was providing them a quality service, but I did not have to work to get their attention. I just did what I enjoyed doing. People took notice and were attracted to what I was doing.

When choosing a business, choose something you can commit to. Business is complicated enough. Don't get stuck doing something you don't like simply because it creates an income. In the long run, it won't likely produce for you anyway, at least not long term. If you're going to get involved in a business that is not connected to your passion and purpose, you might as well stay on your job that you don't like. What's the

If you're going to get involved in a business that is not connected to your passion and purpose, you might as well stay on your job that you don't like.

difference? Don't look at what others are successful at and think it will work for you exactly the same way. Their success could be a reflection of their passion in that particular industry, or they just may be really good at it. Your result may be totally different. Your commitment level will always determine your success level, and you will always be more committed when you are in your own lane. Get back in your lane!

I met a young lady at a pop-up shop that I hosted who was selling jewelry. We spoke about her business. She was very good at telling me all about the company and the product. I even purchased something from her and took her business card to share. Before leaving, I asked her what her real passion was. I don't know where the question came from because based on her presentation, one would think her real passion was selling that jewelry. Something about her and our conversation made me question that. Well, her face lit up! She started talking about how she wanted to make jewelry herself that would make women feel beautiful. She had already decided on the name of her company and some jewelry designs. I thought she spoke with enthusiasm about the company she was presently with, but this was different. She expressed so much excitement just talking about her ideas. She even showed me some pieces in photos on her cell phone that she had made.

Where this young lady was at that time is a great example of how we sometimes reduce our dreams to something basic and easy. We sign up with an already established and known company with a ready-made product, in her case, jewelry. The investment is only $99, and you're in. It's close enough to what you really want to do. I mean, you are selling jewelry. Jewelry is your thing, right? There is nothing wrong with signing up as a distributor with an established company. I know many people who are super successful and have been able to leave their full-time jobs from putting in the work using this model. The issue is when you are stuck there, wanting to do something more, but afraid to take the leap. Just jump and get what God has for you!

Today, this young lady is making jewelry and teaching jewelry-making classes. I am currently working with her to create a system, so she can quickly grow her business, utilizing brand ambassadors to gain exposure for her jewelry line. Was she doing okay before? Yes, of course she was. Is she doing much better now? Definitely! She's walking out her life's purpose and loving each moment. She is having priceless experiences every day in her business and is on her way to quitting her 9 to 5 job. All she had to do was think bigger.

Stop Switching Up

I am sure you know someone who has a new business every six months. Many times, it is an MLM because they are so easy to join. I have a friend who has asked me to join about three or four companies within two years, and she is not with any of them anymore. I remember she got me totally interested in one only because it complimented my business, and when I called her back to discuss it again, she was talking about a different one. Let me be the one to tell you, if it's confusing and irritating to your friends and family, everyone else feels the same way!

In order to be successful at something, you have to stick with it for a while. Success does not come overnight for most of us. It requires time, effort, and consistency. You must be willing to put in the time and the effort to see the success of a thing. We can't always be looking for everything quick and moving on to the next thing when it doesn't happen automatically. You will never get anywhere that way. Pick something and see it through! It can sometimes take years to see significant success in a business. I didn't decide I wanted to be a business coach one day and the next day quit my job. It just doesn't work like that.

As a business owner, you need to establish trust within your target audience. If you are known for switching companies every few months, consumers won't trust that they can count on you to supply their products and will go with someone who is more stable. Also, it is impossible to establish yourself within a target audience if that audience is always changing. It's like starting all over again every time you make a change. If you are spending money on marketing, it becomes a huge waste. Who has money to waste? I can think of a million other ways to spend my money that will actually benefit me and my business.

Everyone is talking about multiple streams of income and encouraging you to create seven or more. That's wonderful! I agree we should have multiple ways of earning money. However, nobody is talking about what that process looks like. This does not mean you should go out there and start ten businesses all at once. The idea is to get something going, get it running smoothly, and then build from it or start something else.

The key part that a lot of people miss is the "get it running smoothly, first" part. How would you ever get the first thing going well if you start something else that will require your time and attention? Your focus becomes divided. It's already divided between your home and business life. Don't forget about church and other volunteer work or whatever else you do. Why add something else to distract you from getting your business in order? Keep in mind also, a stream of income does not always mean creating a business that you have to manage.

One of my coaching clients expressed to me she was ready to create another income source for herself. Because her business was new, and she was still trying to work out some of the kinks, I knew that starting something else would take her focus off her current business, and she would not be able to give it the time and attention it required. I recommended that she create additional income by investing her money. I am not a financial advisor, so I did not advise her how to invest or where to invest, but I encouraged her to do some research. This way she could generate more money without having to give another project her attention. She successfully did that. The following year she worked out most of her business kinks, was a lot more stable in her business, and was ready to start a new project.

She and I sat down, looked at her company and what she was currently doing, and came up with a plan. At the time, she was a makeup artist. I suggested that she incorporate developing her own makeup line and selling it. I also suggested that once she successfully launched her makeup line, to add in distributors to sell her products for her. That was two years ago. Today, she is still helping women to enhance their natural beauty and selling her very own makeup line. She will incorporate distributors later this year. This is a perfect example of multiple streams of income done in such a way that you can actually sustain and grow. What's the point of having multiple streams of income if they are all only generating a few hundred dollars each? Is that the goal?

If in that same scenario, my client would have tried to incorporate developing a makeup line at the beginning of her business, it may have been a flop because she had not yet built up her clientele and perfected how she ran her business. She would have likely made a lot of mistakes that would have cost her money and ruined her reputation, and as I stated in a previous chapter, bad experiences with businesses are memorable, and people can be unforgiving. By growing her business as a makeup artist first, she created an audience for her second business.

Vision Boards and Journaling

To stay committed to your purpose and goals for your business, you need strategies. These strategies should be things that will help you stay on task and also motivate you on those days when you just aren't feeling "it" at all. It must be something that works for you. Not every strategy will work for every business owner. For instance, I do not do well with calendars and planners mainly because I forget about them, especially if they are electronic. I know there are a lot of people who love their calendars. Are you one of those people? It doesn't work for me. I work well with lists, mainly on paper. I have always been a list and note taker. I keep a notebook with various lists and a separate one in

To stay committed to your purpose and goals for your business, you need strategies.

my phone, only to remind me of certain things or to make note of things when I am out and about.

My two favorite and most useful strategies are vision boards and journaling. Creating something purposeful and being able to refer back to it is a great way to keep focus. It helps me to track where I am, where I want to be, and the progress that I am making in the process. Because several other methods were unsuccessful for me, I was thrilled to discover that journaling and vision boards worked so well! So much so that I started to teach a class on vision boards and journaling to show others how amazing this strategy is! So many women have raved about how much they love the idea of a journal and vision board specifically for their business and how it has changed how they pursue their goals.

How many times have you been out doing something completely random not even thinking about your business and had an awesome idea or been in a conversation with someone, and they gave you a piece of really good advice that you "think" will work wonders for your business? Did you write it down? Probably not. Like me, you probably thought this was such a wonderful idea, there would be no way that you would forget. Then, one of your kids called asking what's for dinner, or your boss called about a deadline that you had to meet, and life continued on. A week later, you were watching TV and remembered that you were supposed to be doing something great for your business a week ago.

I would always be awakened in the middle of the night with the absolute best idea ever thought of and say to myself *I will write it down in the morning when I get up*. The problem is by morning I can't remember what it was. All day long, I would be racking my brain trying to remember. Sometimes it comes back to me, and sometimes it is forever lost. I would feel so badly about not remembering because I would pray and ask God for ideas and then not use them. How crazy is that?! The easy solution for this is journaling.

Journaling for me is note-taking on steroids. It has taken my business to new levels over and over again, and it was so simple and inexpensive to implement. I purchased a journal and kept it with me as much as possible. It was even on my bedside table for those middle of the night revelations. When I would have ideas about different parts of my business, I would quickly write them down and all of my associated thoughts about that topic, including the impact it could possibly have on my clients, the pros and cons, the cost, and the potential income and steps to getting it done.

I would also use my journal to document how things were going in my business, such as goal accomplishments, challenges, failures, and new strategies that I would like to implement. This way, I could evaluate what I was doing and make adjustments where they were needed. The best way to learn from your experiences is to document them. Sometimes as business owners, we tend to just keep going and trying things out without properly evaluating what we are doing. This can lead to disappointment and damage to your business and reputation.

Vision boards are by far the best tool for remaining focused and continuously progressing. Having a visual reminder of why I do what I do is so powerful to me. It is a daily reminder of my purpose, and the steps I need to take to fully fulfill that which I was created for. I know a lot of you reading this have made vision boards at some point. However, a lot of people look at vision boards on Pinterest and other sites and think of them as just something pretty to use to show that you would like to have a nice home, a car, and more money. This type of vision board will be of no use to you. It's just something to look at.

Before you sit down with your foam board, glue, and magazines, think about your "why." Why am I here? What is my purpose? What is it I am supposed to be doing? This is how you should always start new projects related to your purpose-driven business. Your "why" should always be at the center of what you are doing. Once you have answered these questions, think about the steps you must take in order to accomplish your purpose. This may include basic things that you may see on other vision boards, such as weight loss, healthier eating, exercise, getting more rest, etc. These things are necessary to achieving success. You must be healthy in order to have energy and strength to do anything. The difference is, you are focused on an end goal. You don't want to be fit just to be able to wear that little red dress even though that's nice, too. When you put more purpose behind something, you are more likely to stick with it.

If you want to be able to confidently share your business with the world, you may put a picture of a nice dress on your vision board to encourage yourself to dress more professionally and to present yourself well to others. Or, if you want to learn more in your particular field to be able to speak and be more knowledgeable, you may select a photo of a cap and gown or school books to express that. Whatever purpose-driven goal you have that is attached to your business, should be expressed on your vision board. It is your vision board. It must motivate you.

I always advise people to create vision boards that focus on short-term goals. You don't have to put your ultimate goal on a vision board. You should focus on the steps that lead to that. This way when you create new vision boards, you can follow the progression. I have so many vision boards, and if I lined them all up in sequence order, you would be able to see how my business has grown and developed over time. I did not rush it. I took my time and went step by step. My current vision board is always on my wall somewhere in my home where I can see it and refer to it on a regular basis.

Your vision board and journal should be extensions of one another. The journal should contain the steps you are taking to reach those goals on the vision board. Again, they should be used together for tracking and understanding where you are and how far you've come.

In my vision board workshops, I guide the participants through the process of deciding what should be included on their vision boards based on their goals. We talk about the use of powerful words that will activate their inner drive and cause them to take action! We go through a very thoughtful process of examining each person's purpose and how they can reach their full potential. In these workshops, I have met so many women who have never set goals for themselves and actually tracked their progress. They just go through the motions every day. After the workshops, they go home with their vision boards, and soon after, they are contacting me. They want to share about how much their daily routines have changed, since they now have something to focus on and to work toward. It really warms my heart and confirms that I am doing the right thing when I hear back from people with such positive feedback of life transformations. Many of these women also form lasting friendships with other participants and continue to encourage one another.

Purpose-Driven Steps

- Think about a mistake in business you have made and what you learned from it.

- Write down two strategies you will implement to help you to stay focused.

- Start keeping a notebook, sticky notes, pad, etc and a pen near you at all times. Watch what amazing ideas will come to you.

- Create a vision board for your business. Place it somewhere where you can see it on a regular basis.

- Purchase a journal to keep with you regularly. Write down specific activities to align with the short-term goals on your vision board.

Chapter 4
Push

We all have challenges and things which can threaten our ability to lead a purposeful life because they tempt us to just simply exist. Sometimes existing feels like a struggle in itself. I have been there. If you haven't, keep living, and you will at some point. For some of us, there are terrible traumatic things that have occurred, and for others, it could just be day-to-day stress that causes days to feel like they are all running together. Either way, we have to be able to bounce back and continue on our path.

One of the things that has helped me to stay focused even through life struggles is to remind myself of why my path matters. When you know that your purpose is connected to other people and can be life-changing for someone else in addition to being life-changing to you, and you know that your purpose is God's plan for your life, you behave differently. That's why having purpose and direction is so important. Without purpose, you don't have any real reason to keep pushing when things get tough. You really could just give up. Why not? Your degree of purpose will determine your degree of push.

While I was writing this book, I was also walking a friend through a process to sobriety. If you have ever loved someone with a serious addiction, you know what that was like for me. If you haven't, I can't even begin to describe it to you. It was the worst! In addition to that, I had my own health issue that came

Without purpose, you don't have any real reason to keep pushing when things get tough.

out of nowhere, and a grandparent who I had spent seven days a week providing care for over the course of a year, passed away. Though she was elderly and not in the best health, it was still unexpected. More stress than a little bit to say the least, but I was able to push through and keep my focus. I am not saying I was like super- woman and didn't fall back a little, because I did. My book was delayed about six weeks because of all of this, but I was able to refocus and jump back in. This book is truly a testimony of pushing through.

    I knew I had a message to share and that it wouldn't get out there until I put it out there! There was too much riding on this project to let it just fall off. You have to find your inner strength to keep going. Life will not wait for you. Everything around you will keep moving. The negativity you see every day that you want to impact in a positive way will keep getting worse until you step up to the plate and solve a problem or meet a need. Nothing is going to happen unless you make it happen.

    You can't entertain the idea of a pity-party, and please don't invite me if you do because I will get on your last nerve. I will do everything in my power to make your pity-party real short. You ever have somebody in your face trying to motivate you, and you just don't want to hear it at all? I know you know what I'm talking about. That is what I'm bringing you! I will help you gain some perspective. There is always someone doing a lot worse than you. That's not to say your situation isn't bad or that you shouldn't feel some type of way about it, but you can't stay there.

When Purpose Shifts

I had the pleasure of talking to one of my very first clients recently. At the time she and I met, she had just started her business and was doing fairly well but wanted to see more growth for her company. I worked with her for three months initially, and then periodically, and watched her business grow over the course of several years. Then, I noticed, I had not seen her on social media anymore or heard from her in a while. I was so accustomed to seeing her posts about her business and giving testimonies, that I immediately noticed her absence. Additionally, she would call me at least once a month, and that came to a halt.

I called her to make sure she was okay, and she explained to me she had stopped doing business because her father was sick and needed more of her attention. Also, her daughter had given birth to her first grandchild, and she wanted to be able to give them whatever free time she had. She was so excited to tell me all about her new grandson and even emailed me some photos.

Her business was going strong for more than eight years, and she really enjoyed it. But, her purpose shifted. This happens sometimes as we go through different phases in life, and not everything is meant to last forever or at least not be exactly the same forever. This does not mean we are not walking in our purpose and have not made an impact. God will elevate us to new levels and call us to do new things. We just have to be able to hear His direction and see His heart for us.

I don't believe letting go of her business was an easy thing for her to do. I am sure there was a lot of prayer and confirmation-seeking involved. She could have hired someone to care for her dad, and she could have spent precious time with her grandchild during her off time, but that wasn't the plan for her life at this time. That doesn't mean she will never get back to her business. It's just not the season for it right now, but I believe if it's God's will, her business will come back with renewed purpose and be even bigger than her first go-round.

For about five years, I brought together women entrepreneurs for networking, hosted mastermind sessions, and provided business support as a part of my coaching business. Over the course of those five years, my audience grew and eventually reached about five hundred members local to me in Maryland and in several other states with women I would interact with online. I often connected members with one another when I felt they could be a great business match. I lead various groups and activities where these women would get together to grow their businesses.

For these five years, I spread the message of women working together in collaboration not competition. This was very refreshing to a lot of people because many business owners had experienced "shade" from other women as they worked to grow and meet new people. Women entrepreneurs were looking for a safe place to interact with other like-minded women where they would receive support and a sense of sisterhood. So, my group was attractive to them. Women quickly became involved and offered support to me in whatever it was I had going on at the time.

When God put it on my heart to write a book, I also knew it was time to give up this part of my business. I felt the transition happening long before I actually gave it up. I absolutely loved organizing these events and working with the ladies. So, when I started to be less enthusiastic about it, I knew that a shift had occurred. Sometimes, God will have to make us not like something anymore in order to take us away from it to give us something bigger. This has happened in my own life many times.

As I mentioned, I was in the educational field, literally since high school. There was nothing else I wanted to do but teach. I loved going to work every day! I had the best time every single day that I walked into my classroom. Then one day, I woke up bored with it. That was the beginning of me becoming an entrepreneur.

I decided to stop organizing events for the group when organizing started to feel too much like work. People were on my nerves, and I was finding myself irritated more than I was enjoying this work that I was once excited to do. God was taking away my love for this, so He could get me to do something else. He had a bigger plan. He did not want me to continue spreading this message on a small scale. It was growth time! When I let it go, I felt a sense of loss because I had worked hard for a long time growing that group and bringing people together. However, now I am seeing how God plans to use that for this next phase. I am also seeing the message continue because the women whom I have worked with have continued to operate from this perspective of women coming together to support one another. Nothing I have done has been lost.

A Closed Door

Doors have closed in my face, and people have told me, "No!" Yes, it is discouraging because we are human, and we like everyone to see what we see and fall in line. However, we have to step out of fantasy land and realize it doesn't always work like that. As awesome as you are, everyone doesn't think so, and everyone is not going to have an interest in your project. That's okay. Just keep it moving.

I am going to share something which will change the way you look at every situation that appears not to be going in your favor! I have trained myself not to be affected when things don't work out in business or any other area of my life. I truly believe that every single thing I am denied was simply not for me, not for me at that time, or not supposed to come in the way I thought it should come. I am not saying that whenever something doesn't come easy, you should give up on it and just accept that it's not for you. I am saying, you should seek God to find out why you did not receive it at that time.

Some years ago, I applied for a director position at a preschool center. I knew I was qualified for the job. I had all the required credentials and experience, and I knew I had done well during the interview. Well, they did not choose me. I was really disappointed because I viewed this as a great opportunity and was really excited about the salary and benefits offered. And, it was much better than what I was being offered by other companies at that time. So, you know my little feelings were hurt!

A couple of weeks later, another company that I had applied with, months prior, called me. They reviewed my resume and wanted to offer me a higher position that I did not apply for. The salary was what I wanted, and they offered great benefits as well. This job was a lot closer to my home than the other one would have been and allowed me to work from home about fifty% of the time, which was amazing! This is also the job that led me to coaching. You see, God had a plan and knew what job I was going to have long before I did. The other job was not the one for me. It was a great opportunity but not *my* opportunity. Two years later, that same preschool center where I thought I wanted to work was on the news for a scandal, and of course, the director's name was all over the news because she was the head of the school. That would have been me—on the news. But, God!

This was a life lesson for me. Now, I look at difficulty and closed doors much differently. Stop crying over a closed door or a difficult situation and seek God. He could be protecting you from something or leading you in another direction.

Rejection in any form is not pleasant. But rejection in business can be especially traumatizing because most of us are super sensitive about our businesses. Our business is our "baby." You have to be able to trust God knows what He's doing, and your steps are ordered.

> *"The steps of a good man are ordered by the Lord: and he delighteth in his way."* Psalm 37:23 (King James Version).

You have to be able to trust God knows what He's doing, and your steps are ordered.

Sometimes, it's not necessarily about rejection, but a lack of opportunity to get our foot in the door that has us stumped. Keep walking in your purpose, and opportunities will come to you. Yes, you have to work and create your own opportunities as well. I am not saying to not do that, but as long as you are in your lane operating in excellence, you will be noticed. I can't tell you how many people have approached me along my journey about speaking at an event or hosting an event in conjunction with individuals on a similar mission just from me minding my business and doing what I do.

Purpose-Driven Steps

- Write down and meditate on three scriptures that encourage you during a rough time.

- Document how your path has changed over time.

- Write down examples of times when a door was closed, or you got a "No," and you later realized it was for your good.

Chapter 5

Connections that Count

To do business, your brain has to be set on success but not just your success. You have to be willing to cultivate relationships and help someone else to win. Also, you must believe in their purpose and support their dreams. This does not only apply to business. This can be applied to your personal life as well. You can help someone win in their marriage, in raising their children, and in their career. Utilize whatever area where you have had some success and pass it on to someone else. That person who you help will be a forever friend to you. They will even start to pour into you in areas where they have had success, and the roles will reverse. That's how you will know you have sown into good ground. All relationships should be give and take. Remember, that if a person is not adding to you, they are in some way taking from you. This applies to your contribution in the relationship as well.

Forming Your Circle of Support

Okay, let's get back to business. Have you ever been a part of a business group on social media or some other forum and noticed that everyone is there to promote their business, and nobody is really growing as a result of that group? Well, that is because everyone is selling. Nobody is buying. What would happen in that same group if everyone changed their perspective and instead of asking, *"What can be done for me?"*, decided to ask, *"How can I support you?"* I think it's possible for

To do business, your brain has to be set on success but not just your success.

many more women to actually grow their business using this type of strategy.

When you go back to your social media group, do something different. Instead of posting your business, ask if anyone has a new product they would like to share. Buy something from someone. Share their product or service with someone else and encourage them to buy. Go to their website or page and leave a positive review of the product. A couple of things will take place when you do this as a routine. You will meet new women in business who can become part of your circle of support. These women will feel supported, and some of them will turn around and support you. I can tell you from experience that this works, and it works a lot better than pushing your products in every conversation. People don't generally like a pushy sales person and will start to hide from you.

A couple of years ago, I decided to start doing vendor events to provide a place for other business owners to share their products and to put some money in my own pocket. Yes, it's ok to consider your own pocket. During the vendor event, I made a point to go around to each table and get to know each business owner. I learned about their business and about them as a person. Well, as much as I could in a short period of time. I also bought things from their tables. I can honestly say that each of those women who I took the time to support have come back and supported me. I made ten new connections, supported ten businesses, and gained ten new customers on the spot and in the weeks to follow. Eight out of ten of these women I still communicate with on a regular basis, and we support one another's businesses consistently.

I call them my circle of support. These are the women who I can share ideas with, get advice from, and collaborate with. Having a circle of support is much better than having a customer! Customers come and go. They move on to other shiny products and forget about yours. They must be maintained and retained. A circle of support is the backbone of your business. Your circle of support will ride with you regardless of the next new thing hitting the market. They form your inner circle in business. The circle can be as large as you are willing to grow it. Some refer to this group of supporters as your tribe.

Would I have had the same outcome if I had set up a vendor table myself and focused on selling my products instead of supporting them? Not likely. I had to train my mind to always consider someone else. This is different than considering someone else above yourself. My needs were always considered. I am always working as my own biggest advocate. I had already figured out that by supporting another woman, I was building my own business. By no means am I telling you not to focus on your own goals and not to go hard for yourself. I am helping you to see there may be a more effective way to reach the level of success you desire.

The Approach to Forming Your Circle of Support

What I want for you is to experience having an inner circle or circle of support in the way that I have. Navigating through new relationships can be challenging because a lot of people are not sincere, and many are super self-serving. Add business and money into the mix, and it can be exhausting and disappointing at times. The way most of us connect nowadays is through social media and networking events that we learn about on social media. The best way to widen your circle is to reach out but be selective. Follow people who are doing what you are doing or what you want to do, and people who have skills that you need for business. If you notice that someone is great at social media advertising, and you are lacking in that area, reach out to that person. Send them a quick message. "Hey, I noticed you online. I think you have a great social media presence and was wondering if you had an online course I could take part in that would help me grow my business?" Or "Hello, I'm inviting a group of local women entrepreneurs to meet for lunch to see how we can all help one another grow. Would you like to attend?" Most women in business want to connect with others and would be open to an invite. Some won't. Don't worry about them. Keep it moving and invite someone else. You can't be turned off by someone else's "shade." Just send them a copy of my book.

When meeting new people, you should always put your best foot forward, but please don't pretend like you have it all together. Being fake is recognized right away and is the number one relationship crusher. Nobody likes that! You can't trust a person who is always being someone else in your presence. This definitely applies to business as well. Be confident in your purpose and always walk in that confidence no matter where you are in the process. Let other people be great in the areas where they thrive and ask them for help. Let them make you better. I seek out friends who are smarter than me about certain things. The beauty is I now have more than just my own knowledge to work with. I can benefit and grow from what they know. It would never benefit me to pretend like I know everything, or like I am good at everything and not utilize the skills present within my circle. It would only stop me from operating my business at its best.

Be an Opportunist

Other people are connected to us for different reasons. We have made the word "opportunist" to mean something negative thanks to reality TV. However, it's actually not. I am an opportunist, and you should be, too. I do look for opportunities within situations and take full advantage of them. If you're not looking for opportunities, trust me, they won't be banging your door down! Many people miss their chance simply out of fear of looking like an opportunist and not seeking out what they need to be successful.

    When I am first getting to know someone, I take my time and learn things about them. I take the same time to share things about myself. In that time, I am learning what they like to do, what they do well, how they can contribute to my life, and how I can contribute to theirs. There are women in my life who are great at things I struggle with. I don't have time to learn everything. I'd rather stay in my lane and let them shine in their lane. You must be mature enough to let someone else shine in your presence. Remember, you aren't the only one with a gift from God, and why "shade" someone for doing something that you won't do anyway? For instance, why be jealous of someone who is killing the competition is sales, and you have no desire to sell products? Let them have that!

    Some of the women I meet are in my life strictly for spiritual accountability. Others are in my life because we connect on a business level, and our talents complement one another. Then, there are those who I just like to hang out with because they are super positive and keep me motivated to do well and be well. You may run into trouble when you start interchanging roles. Everything is not for everybody. If you are expecting something of me that I don't have to give, we will not have a successful friendship or business relationship, and if I have unrealistic expectations of you, I will always be disappointed. You must know who each person is and what their purpose is in your life.

Sometimes, we give indiscriminately to someone, and at the moment they are unable to give anything to us. Maybe they're in a crisis. Even in crisis, other people can give to us. Maybe God wants to deal with you in an area of your life where you can grow and is using another person to get you to a new level of winning! I have certain business associates who I am always pouring into. I understood early on that this was my role with them. I was ok with pouring and pouring because I knew the purpose of it. God wanted them to win and wanted to use me to get them there. I also understood that somehow, someway, I would also receive from my obedience. It turns out that most of them have referred new clients to me this past year. They got what they needed from me, and I also grew my business, but I never charged them a dime for what I was pouring out.

Everyone is Not For You

I try to get along with most people, but not everyone is meant to be my friend, and not everyone is meant to do business with me. If your friendship or business relationship is too much work or stress for me, I must let you go. Your stress will cause me to lose focus and hinder my dream-building. Sometimes, you have to move on from people, but it doesn't have to be a negative experience. There is no need for eye-rolling and teeth-sucking whenever you see this person. Just simply move on and do it without talking bad about this person to other people. You don't have to expose the spot on her crown to everyone. Let God clean her up in private. Does He expose all your mess? Has He exposed any of your mess? Okay.

In the same way, I am not for everyone. Not everyone can work with me. Not everyone will like me. Guess what? That's ok! Business relationships can be tricky and require a good foundation and connection. If you don't have that, it's ok not to proceed. When choosing a business coach or partner in business, approach it like you would approach choosing a counselor. Simply put, there are people who you connect better with and will be more open to. You will also be able to work with them with less stress. If the chemistry isn't right, refer them to someone else and walk away.

Recently, an associate of mine came to me with a business idea and an invitation to join him in his new venture. I took the idea to a mutual friend to ask her what she thought about it. She said to me something that made so much sense. She said, "I don't think it is a good idea for the two of you to go into business together because you both have very different relationships with money." This woman knows me very well and knows I am not a money-hungry person. She knows I am not willing to sacrifice my beliefs and principles for a dollar. She knows I am not out to just make the highest dollar at any cost. She also knows that the other person may be more willing to do so if the price were right. She was absolutely correct, we should not be business partners. Our business morals did not match. Can you imagine that fight? It would have been super stressful for us to deal with one another on a regular basis, and when you add money into the equation, watch out! It would have been war, and the business would not have succeeded. I'm so glad I spoke to her about it first, and I am so glad I have people who can speak into my life and help me avoid unforeseeable mistakes.

Don't operate with the mentality of, "If I miss this opportunity another one may not come." Don't be desperate. Desperation will put you in a position of vulnerability every time! You will be vulnerable to whatever scheme comes along. It is much better to wait on the right opportunity than to have to dig your way out of the wrong one. The opportunity you avoid is most likely not connected to your purpose anyway. Ask God to reveal to you what His plans are. That is where your purpose lies and those who are connected to it.

Don't operate with the mentality of, "If I miss this opportunity another one may not come."

"Many are the plans in a person's heart, but it is the Lord's purpose that prevails." Proverbs 19:21 (New International Version)

Accountability

Many of us cringe at the word accountability because it forces us to do something. It forces us not to make excuses and end up in the same place next month as we're in this month. It forces us to step outside of our comfort zone and take action that will lead us somewhere. However, on the flip side, some of us are searching for an accountability partner because we realize the value and importance of having

someone to play this role in our lives. It is so important! If you want to fully live in your purpose, you need to be held accountable by someone whom you trust. This person will check in with you, encourage you, assist you, motivate you, and hopefully also pray with you.

When selecting this person, it is critical not to just jump out there and choose someone randomly or just because they are a friend of yours. Think about what you specifically need from this person and who you may know that has the qualities you're looking for. This person may not be one of your friends. It may be someone you know from church, a business associate, a mentor, etc. Everyone's needs and communication styles are different and should be taken into consideration.

I have served as an accountability partner for many people. In some cases, we were accountability partners for one another. In other cases, it was one-sided. In both instances, I greatly benefitted from the relationship. It was great to be able to receive support from the person whom I was giving my support to, but it also made my heart happy to just help someone else reach a goal. I think I play that role most often, especially as a coach.

When selecting an accountability partner for myself, I knew I needed someone who I could relate to on a spiritual and business level because I needed them to be able to relate to me as I worked on my business goals, and I also needed them to be able to believe God with me. Once I found my perfect match, I was set, and she is still my accountability partner to this day five years later.

My accountability partner and I communicate via text at least twice a week. It works perfectly because we are both busy, and we are both ok with communicating this way. We also meet in person once each month to enjoy a good meal and talk about things we discussed during the month. When she finds things related to my business, such as good articles, promotional packages, etc., she sends them to me.

When a scripture makes her think of me, she sends me that, too, and it is usually just what I needed in that moment. Our relationship forces me to do what I need to do because I want to be able to say I accomplished the weekly goal whenever we talk. I'm laughing now thinking about the conversations we've had as I've been writing this book!

Purpose-Driven Steps

- List three types of business owners who you would like to make connections with.

- Write down some strategies you will use to network more effectively.

- Name two people who can serve as potential accountability partners for you and why you would choose them. Then, approach them with your goals and the partnership proposal.

Chapter 6

It's Not Just YOU!

In my years of coaching and networking with other women entrepreneurs, I have heard some of the same scenarios of challenges and let downs over and over again, and each time the person is thinking, "Is it just me?!" No. It's not just you. Many of us have had the same experiences as we embark on our business ventures. We share many of the same challenges and disappointments and have had to work through some of the same kinks. The key is how we handle those situations. We should not allow these challenges to make us quit! *"But as for you, be strong and do not give up, for your work will be rewarded."* 2 Chronicles 15:7 (NIV)

Like most people who decide to go into business, I have had both good and bad days. I have also learned a lot about myself and other people during this process. What I have learned about myself is that I am stronger than my circumstances, and I have the ability to bounce back from a failure or a mistake. I have also learned, people will not always respond to you the way you think they will living in your purpose. This is why you must establish early on and be confident with your life of entrepreneurship, so you won't be deterred from the path based on people.

Not everyone will be interested in what you have going on, and not everyone is passionate about the thing that drives you. You have to be okay with that and keep going. Doors will close in your face. People will be fake and talk behind your back. People will even purposely try to sabotage you. I know that sounds scary, but I don't mean to scare you. My goal is to equip you for what's really real out here! You must remember though that nobody and nothing can stop your purpose unless you surrender it to them

> "No weapon formed against you shall prosper, and every tongue which rises against you in judgement you shall condemn." Isaiah 54:17 (New King James Version)

When Your Family and Friends Don't Support You

This is one of the biggest challenges I hear most often. I also think it is the one that hurts the most because you don't see it coming. You have an expectation that the people you love will support your dreams and be your biggest cheerleaders. When that doesn't happen, it hits you right in the gut. It can make you question your purpose and what you're doing because if your own family won't support you, who will? It can rob you of your confidence and cause you to shrink back.

Let me explain why sometimes family and friends do not support your dreams or not in the way you might expect. Before you discovered your purpose and knew the path you should take, they knew you. They knew you when you were a different person. They have seen you go through the various phases of life. It may be difficult for them to see you in this new light. They are too familiar. Does this make sense? Is it

You must remember though that nobody and nothing can stop your purpose unless you surrender it to them.

right? No. Is it true? Definitely, so! For some of your family members and friends, they may prefer you when you're not living in your purpose. Your being so great may be a reminder to them of their own failures and what they did not accomplish. It also may give you less time to cater to them and their needs. Therefore, it may be hard for them to celebrate with you because they are losing something.

In everything I have done in business, except for a core group, I have always received more support from strangers and people I have met in networking than from my family and close friends. When I hosted events, those closest to me would not even respond to the invite, and this would happen on multiple occasions. I'm talking once a month or every other month. After a while, I just stopped inviting them. But, guess what? I still had a packed room of people who found value in what I was doing. I was fortunate to have some friends and family join in, but they were typically those who were entrepreneurs themselves. I think it makes a difference when you understand and respect the hustle.

I am very real with myself, and I know for a fact many of my family members will never pick up this book to read it and will never attend an event to support me. I have to be ok with that because the alternative is to dwell on it and allow it to slow me down. Not happening! You cannot be moved by what other people do, and you cannot find self-value in what someone else chooses to value, even if it's your mama! I am blessed that that is not my story, but I have heard that story many times. My mother was spreading the word about this book at the hospital where she works before it even got to the publisher.

When I first went into business, one of the things I knew I had to do right away, was to make some new friends. The friends and family I had were wonderful, and I love and value them, but I needed people in my life who understood the grind of entrepreneurship. If you fail to surround yourself with people on a similar path, you will be disappointed trying to make other people understand the grind. This means I had to widen my circle quite a bit. I knew I would need a different kind of support that the people in my life at the time would not be equipped to provide.

Your family members, like mine, may tell you to just get a job, secure a check, and retire. They mean well, and they think they are telling you the right thing. But, if you're goal is full time self-employment, you don't need this in your ear constantly. You need to be around people who will consistently feed your passions. I am not saying to stay away from your family. By all means, please maintain these connections unless they are totally unhealthy for you. What I am saying is, choose what to discuss with them. Don't talk about your business to people who don't understand and might lead you into a debate about it. Talk about things with them which will allow you both to enjoy the time spent. The funny thing is once you start to reach your goals and achieve success, all of a sudden everyone will respect your decision.

People who I know, "clowned me" and joked about me writing this book. That is because they are not familiar with me as a business coach and a writer. They were not a part of that world with me. I was just their cousin, aunt, sister, daughter, granddaughter, niece, friend, etc. They had never taken part in this other segment of my life and didn't really know what I did professionally. A lot of them thought I was still teaching children. Regardless of that, did I not write this book and is it not good? Am I not a very successful 100% self-employed business coach? Of course, after all the joking, they were supportive of my accomplishment and very happy for me.

To Leave or Not to Leave?

I have never met an entrepreneur who did not dream of or at least have an interest in being able to leave their full- time employment to do business. Who wouldn't want to own all their time to spend it how they please and be totally financially free? However, this is something you have to work up to, and it definitely doesn't occur over night.

Your family members, like mine, may tell you to just get a job, secure a check, and retire.

For most people, it doesn't even occur over the course of a couple of years. So, we stay at our jobs for the steady paycheck, since we have steady bills, health insurance, and the promise of a retirement check.

I do not recommend that any entrepreneur lets go of stable employment prior to their business reaching the level where it is producing at least what they were earning from their job and is steadily increasing and has been for a period of time. Experts say you need to earn 1.5 times the amount you are making on your current job to cover costs, such as health insurance, self-employment taxes, insurance, and others. So, if you're making $85,000 a year in your current job, you'll need to secure $127,500 annually to cover these costs. Of course, the exception would be that God Himself has directed you to make this move sooner. I don't want to discourage anyone from stepping out in faith. However, I want you to use wisdom. If you are married, please talk this over with your spouse prior to taking this leap, especially if you desire to stay married.

My situation was a little different. My job ended, and I just didn't look for another one. I had been doing business for a little while and was ok with where I was financially. I decided at that time to just make the transition. That was about five years ago. Since then, I have remained active in the education field, periodically, working contracts through my coaching business.

Even though the way I made the transition was not something I pondered over for months and months, carefully planning each move. It worked for me, and I had complete peace about it. I knew I was walking in God's plan for my life even though everyone thought I was completely crazy. As a rule of thumb, I don't recommend you go about it the way I did. "Do as I say and not as I do," as my mom used to say. I still don't quite know what that means.

When doing business and working a full-time job, you must be super creative with your time. Please keep in mind that the company you are working for is paying you to work for them not to work your business. Be respectful. It is not honorable to use their time and supplies for your business. Stop using their copier to print your business cards and their computer to design your website. Remember, you will someday be paying staff if you grow large enough and will want them to give you that same respect.

As a working entrepreneur, I had to stay up late at night to finish things and work on weekends. Whatever it took to get the job done, I had to do that. I still met all my deadlines at work and gave them my full attention when I was there on their clock. I had to meet with clients after hours and on Saturdays for a couple of years which was fine because most of them were working entrepreneurs, also. You can make it work and remain honorable to your job.

I don't know about you, but I would really be irritated when people would call my business a side hustle. Even when I was working my business in addition to having a job, it was never a side hustle for me. It was always a top priority of mine and was always a reflection of my purpose. I wasn't about to let people diminish my business to something insignificant. I would always correct them and say, "This is not just something I do on the side!" Entrepreneurs with side hustles will always have just a side hustle. If that's all you can see, that's all you can have.

Purpose-Driven Steps

- Think about some challenges you have faced and how you were able to get past them. Was there anything you could have done differently?

- Write a list of people who are very supportive of you. This will remind you of what is important when you come across someone who is not supportive.

- Write down how much money you would need to earn in order to leave your full-time job if you desired to using the 1.5 multiplier. Create small goals to help you reach that figure.

Chapter 7

The Invisible Business

It is vitally important to the success of your business to get it in front of your target audience. People need to know that you exist. The more exposure you gain, the better. Today, I see a lot of business activity on social media which is great but not effective if it doesn't reach its target. Be sure to connect with your intended audience. It's ok to share with everyone in general because even if they have no need for your business, they may know someone who does and could provide a great referral or two, but you should be purposefully interacting with those who you know for certain have an interest. How do you know if they have interest?

An issue that I have seen is some entrepreneurs aren't clear on who their audience is. Figuring this out is one of the main components to the startup process. You should establish who your customer is at the very beginning, so you can tailor your business to meet their needs, even as those needs may change over time. This is how you retain customers.

Here is the fundamental question any entrepreneur should ask themselves if they want to be successful in business, "What problem does your product or service solve, and who may need that product or service?" When you are able to express that you meet a need or solve a problem, you capture the attention of those who have that problem or need. From that point, you have to establish what makes you

People need to know that you exist.

different from others who solve that problem or meet that need because you may not be the only one.

There are a lot of business coaches out there, and what I do is quite different from what I have seen other coaches do. For this reason, I decided to drop the title business coach this year and go with something that better reflects what I actually do: Purpose Coaching. I still work primarily with business owners, however, but from the perspective of creating a purpose-driven business not just a successful money-maker. Entrepreneurs who are just in it for the money aren't my target audience. I work with those who want to think bigger, live from their purpose, and express their passion. I express this in everything I put out to the public, even on social media.

Keep in mind the way people connect on different social media platforms varies, but your strategy should be the same. Make connections, especially with people who will invest in you and don't waste time chasing down those who won't. I am not saying to avoid an intentional strategy to acquire clients, but if you are harassing people, it's just not a good look and will almost never lead to anything positive. Keep your message consistent and be professional. If you can do this and develop a reputation for quality work and dependability, you will see growth in your business.

I frequently receive inbox messages from a woman who sells life insurance. I already have life insurance and have no need of her services. I've told her this numerous times, and yet she continues to message me at least once a month. This past week, I blocked her. Now, if I ever need life insurance in the future or wanted to refer someone for a policy, I would not choose her because she irritated the heck out of me! I would not invite her to any of my networking events because I wouldn't want her to come and start bothering other guests.

If your only business presence is social media, you are doing yourself a disservice. Have you noticed the changes that have recently occurred with business visibility on social media platforms? Things are changing. Do you want to leave it up to Facebook to get your business out there? You have to explore alternatives and engage your audience in multiple ways. Many business owners are doing radio interviews, being featured in magazines, and posting YouTube videos, etc. to get their business noticed.

A common mistake I see business owners do is to only have pages on social media and not their own website. The problem with this is you don't control social media. You need your own platform where you are in control of your content and who it can be shared with. It also establishes the fact you are a legitimate business. I would never trust a business that only exists on Facebook and Twitter. I would be very reluctant to give you more than about $25 for anything because I need to know I can find you later if you have my money, and I need to get it back from you for whatever reason. If you won't make the investment in your business to have a website, why would anyone want to invest in you by spending their money with you?

When I host events, I share them online, but I also contact agencies that could benefit from my services and encourage them to attend as well. I reach out to the local community in the area where my event is being held and get other businesses involved. I even take my show on the road and offer the same event in multiple states. As a result, I am able to spread the word and fill the seats. I may not have received the same result with just a few Facebook posts.

Sharing vs. Selling

Some people are just amazing at sales and can get anyone to purchase anything, even stuff they don't really want. They are just that good! These types of people can do well with both product and service-based businesses. Have you ever been sucked into buying a time share or a car that was more expensive than what you set out to spend? Chances are you had an encounter with a really good sales rep who was on a mission to get you to sign your name on the dotted line.

I personally do not like selling. I don't like to have to persuade someone to do business with me. The beautiful thing about it is I don't have to and neither do you. You must learn to *share* your business not *sell* your business. Sharing is different from selling but has the same outcome. I tell people about my business everywhere I go, and not just for the purpose of convincing them to work with me. I share from the perspective that I offer a great service which will benefit them. Based on my conversation with them over a short period of time, I am able to express to them ways they can enhance their lives and their business by working with me. I discover their need and share with them how I can meet that need. I am not selling them anything. I am just telling them what I do. I have never sold anything to my clients.

Another super important thing to remember is people like connections. In many cases, a person will spend with you because they like you and connect with you on certain levels. Be likeable! If you could only take away one thing from this book, that should be it. Make people like you! You will be able to touch more people with your gift and make much more money. I can say with confidence, more than half of my clients work with me and pay me good money because they like me. They liked me first. Then, they trusted me and learned what I could do for them. This method will create for you clients for life and subsequent referrals.

If you find that you are selling and selling and selling, and it feels pushy to you, know that it feels pushy to them, also. Sit down and think about the value in your product or service and decide how you will share that value with others.

Why You're Really Afraid to Tell People About Your Business

The absolute most puzzling thing I have ever heard from a client was that they did not post about their business because they did not want people "all in their business." This one surprised me! I was even more surprised to hear it more than once from multiple people. I asked one of my clients to explain this to me. Her business was product-based and would likely do well online, but she did not post about it on her social media pages. Her answer blew me away! She stated she did not want people in her business. By people, she meant family and friends. I asked her to repeat herself, so I could make sure I was hearing her correctly. This client and a few others expressed wanting to keep their business private from the people they know. As I stated before, it is very unfortunate that many family members will not support your business. However, it makes zero sense to keep quiet about your business because you anticipate you will not be supported. How will you ever make any money with a secret business? After a lot of thought and processing, I came up with my theory on the root of this issue.

In a previous chapter, I talked a little bit about doing everything in excellence and having a business you can be proud of. I think, not wanting to share your business with certain people is due to a lack of confidence in your business, your product, or your service. If you are concerned about the people you know following your business, it's time to go back and get your business tightened up. This may require you to revamp your product, change how you deliver your services, or redo your website etc. Do what you need to do to feel good about it. Confidence is key. When you lack confidence, it shows, and people won't trust your business.

Another reason why I think people don't want those closest to them to know about their business is because, as I mentioned before, they are afraid they will fail. Nobody looks forward to failing, and what makes failing worse is when everyone knows about it. This has kept me quiet in the past, which helps me recognize this issue when I see this same fear in other people. So, you have decided if you are going to fail, you will fail in private. Unfortunately, you have guaranteed your failure by thinking this way! You don't even believe in your own purpose. Why should anyone else? You have decided before you even got started this will not be a success and have already established your defense mechanism.

When you lack confidence, it shows, and people won't trust your business.

You cannot be successful at a business nobody knows about. You need your exposure to reach as far and wide as possible to increase your chances of drawing in more and more clients or customers. You can't reach new levels if you haven't conquered level one. Get over your fear of people and their opinions and go after what is yours! God has laid it out for you. It's all there within your reach. Are you really going to let fear keep you paralyzed? Do you really want to look back next year and be in the exact same position as today? How many people would never be reached with something they need because you did not believe in your purpose enough to run with it?

Purpose-Driven Steps

- Develop two new strategies for sharing your business—whether via social media or an external community or platform.

- Identify areas of fear in your life which have hindered you from sharing your business and expel those areas!

- Make a list of all the people who will be positively impacted by your business and begin outreach.

.

Bonus Chapter

Becoming a Woman of Purpose

Being a woman of great purpose is a big responsibility because people are always watching your every move. Some are watching for guidance, and others are watching to catch you slipping. That's just real! To some, this means you must always be "on." To me, it just means I need to be mindful. Being "on" implies that what I do and who I am is an act. There is no acting here. I am always me. You are always going to get the same person no matter where or how you encounter me. That's all I know how to be. I am very mindful that my actions affect other people and have the ability to steer people in the right or wrong direction, and I don't take that lightly. I just strive day to day to be the best me.

Walking in purpose also requires a commitment. People will want your time, attention, and energy, and sometimes those people don't consider that you are human and have a personal life, a family, and other responsibilities. I am at a good place in my life right now as a single person without children. I actually have a little more time to devote to my mission and pouring into others. At the same time, I value personal space and time, and I make sure that I prioritize "me" time.

I have had to learn over the years how to separate myself from my business in order to take care of me. If I don't, I will quickly become burned out and

Bonus Chapter | 107

You are always going to get the same person no matter where or how you encounter me.

will be of no use to anyone. If I am not a happy and whole person, how can I truly tune into my purpose, and what will I truly have to offer someone else? I take time for myself each month without fail. I don't care what is happening around me. I am getting that time! I get a pedicure, a massage, and a day completely to myself. I am not rushing around that day. I am not taking care of other people that day, and I am not working that day.

Having time to myself gives me renewed energy to continue. It's also great thinking time. I can reflect on my recent moves and what I plan to do next. Yes, I know I said I am not working that day, but I can't turn off thinking. I am an entrepreneur. You know our brains don't turn off. I'm just not taking business calls, updating websites, or checking social media. The peace of it all is very beneficial and healthy. If you are not getting that time in, please incorporate it into your routines immediately.

You don't have to spend your time the way I spend mine. You may want to just stay home and not be bothered that day. Do that! Whatever makes you feel relaxed should be how you spend your day. The people in your life should respect that time and leave you alone! This may take practice, especially if you are married and/or have children. Get them on board and do you!

All the Single Ladies!

Being single without children does not mean you are 100% available to everyone all the time. Single women, please don't fall into that trap. A lot of people think that single women, especially those of us who have not yet had children, have nothing to do but cater to other people. I have had to correct people often and let it be known that I am working on something and going somewhere! I don't have time to babysit everyone's children, to run people's errands, or to be anyone's personal taxi driver. Single does not mean "available for part time work," and it certainly doesn't mean purposeless. I am busy. I have my own life, and I'm not looking for things to do.

I am all for offering a helping hand and doing things for others as an expression of love. What I am saying is I can't devote all my weekends to helping you organize your closets, take your braids out, or run you around to do all your errands. If I do that, I am not putting in enough time toward God's vision for my own life. There will be something lacking in my life because I am too busy helping everyone else manage their life.

I hope every single woman who has discovered her purpose will get real comfortable telling people, "I love you but no."

Single does not mean "available for part time work," and it certainly doesn't mean purposeless.

You can't always provide a yes for everything. You won't get where you need to be. It took me a long time to get to this place of being comfortable saying no, and now I am able to live purposefully every day. I still have plenty of family time and still go the extra mile for the people I love, but it does not come between me and my goals! Speaking of goals, please know it is much easier to reach your goals when you have educated yourself. I watch entrepreneurs fail to invest in their business education all the time. You can't just jump in and go with the flow. You must be prepared to create the flow. It amazes me when I post on social media that I am hosting a business education event and have slots open for vendors, how quickly I get flooded with inquiries about the vendor opportunity. Responses for actual participants in the educational event come in much slower. Why is that? People see vendor opportunities as a way to make money. They place value on that opportunity. However, they don't place the same value on a learning experience that will generate much more income over time because they can't see past immediate gratification. Everybody wants that quick dollar! Please, do away with this thinking and invest in yourself. It will serve you in ways that a vendor opportunity will not. The goal is continued income not a one-time event.

A Final Word

You are a woman of great purpose fully equipped to walk out your purpose and affect change, which ultimately fulfills God's plan in the earth for His people. You have what it takes, and you are enough. It's time you believe that and take the first step. It's going to be an amazing journey full of ups and downs, loops, and turns, but it will be well worth it. Remember, mistakes are learning experiences, and sometimes God will have to take you out of your comfort zone to get you to a new position. Trust the process. Trust yourself, and most of all, trust the One who created you with purpose. Now, go, believe in, and walk in your purpose!

Ready to be a Purpose-Driven Entrepreneur? Not sure where to start?

I hope my book has inspired you to start thinking about or to think more deeply about your purpose and how it aligns with your business aspirations and goals. I would love to chat with you sometime and follow your progress as you continue in your journey.

If you would like to connect with me beyond the pages of this book, I invite you to join my mailing list at **shanniwilke.com** for weekly inspiration, tips, and tools to guide you in your business endeavors and encouragement when you need a little push.

Bonus Chapter | 113

There you will also find other resources you may take advantage of, such as webinars, online business coaching, and in-person group coaching sessions.

Glossary of Terms

Brand

A product or service that is distinguishable from other products, services, or concepts.

Brand Ambassador

A person who is hired by an organization to increase awareness of a brand. The brand ambassador is meant to embody the brand identity in appearance, demeanor, values, and ethics.

Brand Message

Every communication that makes a customer relate to the brand. It influences and motivates a customer to buy from the brand.

Core Values

The fundamental beliefs of a person or organization.

Distributor

A member of a non-salaried work force which sells a company's product or service earning a commission for themselves.

Gifts

God-given abilities and talents.

Purpose

The reason for which something is done or created.

Target Audience

A particular group for which a product or service was created.

ZION Publishing House is a family-owned publishing company based in Southern California and Washington, DC. ZION helps Christian authors tell their stories by providing an affordable alternative to traditional publishing. Our mission is to maintain a platform that educates and empowers independent Christian authors. We do this by cultivating talent in the inspirational and self-help genres for novice and experienced authors. The path to publishing can be daunting and extremely complex. We take pride in taking our clients by the hand and walking them through the publishing process to ensure they not only have a high-quality product that resonates with the reader, but they understand the many facets of the publishing industry and what it means to be a published author.

If you are a writer looking for an affordable path to publishing, visit our website at www.zionpublishinghouse.com to learn more.

www.ingramcontent.com/pod-product-compliance
Lightning Source LLC
Chambersburg PA
CBHW030329080526
44584CB00012B/777